THOMAS HEATHERWICK:

DESIGNER

Claire Llewellyn

OXFORD
UNIVERSITY PRESS

CONTENTS

DAILY NEWS

27 July 2012

LONDON WOWS THE WORLD!

2012 Olympics open in style in London

The London 2012 Olympic Games were officially opened by the Queen last night. The four-hour extravaganza included the Parade of Nations, featuring all 204 teams. The evening ended with the lighting of the Olympic cauldron, the most important symbol of the Games. It was a stunning finale.

The Olympic flame

The cauldron stands at the centre of the stadium and is formed from 204 elements made of polished copper. Each copper element represents a different nation and was brought into the stadium by its team during the Parade. The copper elements were fixed to long metal stems that spread out flat on the ground. At a little past midnight, the Olympic flame arrived in the stadium carried by seven young athletes and the cauldron was lit.

Symbol of unity

To the gasps of the 80 000 spectators, the lit copper elements began to rise gently on their metal stems. Wave after wave of burning petals lifted upwards, forming a single great flame in the centre. It was a heart-stopping moment: a symbol of the peaceful unity of nations. The beautiful cauldron will now keep burning throughout the Games. It was made by British designer, Thomas Heatherwick.

WHO IS THOMAS HEATHERWICK?

THE MAN

Thomas Heatherwick has run Heatherwick Studio, his own London-based design studio, for over 20 years. He is different from many other designers. He is part-architect, part-designer, part-inventor and part-sculptor and has produced a wide range of products that are original, artistic and even a little bit odd!

THE PROJECTS

Most of the projects that Thomas works on are for the public. They include:

- a brand new, fuel-saving London bus
- a canal footbridge that rolls up to allow boats to pass
- a pair of sculptures that double as air vents for an electricity station
- a new garden bridge over the River Thames.

These projects are not just decorative: they have a useful function and each one is unique.

Thomas is fascinated by materials – plastics, wood, ceramics and glass. He spent many years learning to work with them, and uses them in his projects in unusual ways. Unlike many other design studios, Heatherwick Studio has a workshop where ideas are tested. Can a wooden wall bend without a hinge? How will a handrail feel to the touch? The workshop finds the answers.

This book is all about Thomas Heatherwick. It describes his family life, childhood and long years of training. It explains his personal vision and the way he tackles his designs. It looks inside Heatherwick Studio and at the people who work with him. Finally, it discusses some of his projects and sets them side by side with other interesting designs from around the world.

FAMILY LIFE

Thomas Heatherwick was born in 1970. He grew up in a large rambling house in north London. His family was very creative and everyone had strong personal interests. They introduced Thomas to design and to making from an early age.

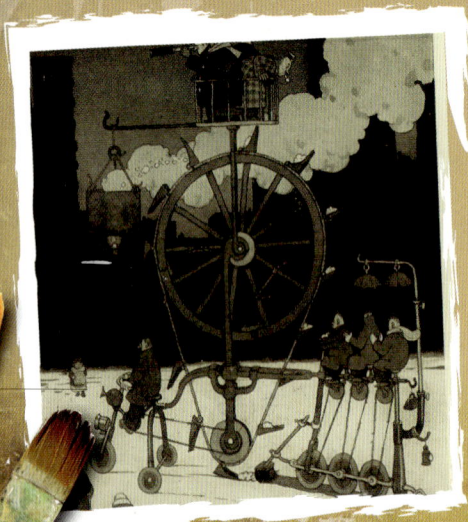

His grandfather, Miles, was a musician and writer. He:

- was fascinated by engineers, such as Isambard Kingdom Brunel
- was interested in mechanical things and collected model trains
- loved cartoons by William Heath Robinson of crazy complex inventions.

His grandmother, Elisabeth, was an artist. She:

- designed and painted fabrics
- set up the fabric design studio of the chain store, Marks and Spencer; her fabrics were worn by people up and down the country
- was interested in beauty: she believed that art, colour and pattern made people feel better.

His mother, Stefany, is also an artist. She:

- is a painter, jeweller and an expert on beads
- designed and made jewellery at the family home
- ran a shop selling necklaces and beads for over 20 years
- has a passion for crafts and craftsmanship.

MY MUM'S WORKROOM WAS FULL OF CHEMICAL POWDERS AND KILNS, AND LOTS OF WIRE AND PLIERS – TOOLS EVERYWHERE.
T.H.

His father, Hugh, is a community worker. He:

- is a trained pianist
- has worked with groups of children and adults to help them become more creative
- has studied how children develop and flourish
- is excited by new ideas such as new design, new housing and the future of cities.

GOING OUT WITH MUM

Thomas went with his mother to the craft fairs where she showed and sold her work. He wandered around and talked to other craftspeople: glass-blowers, blacksmiths, metal-workers and embroiderers. He watched them skilfully using tools to make pots, lay hedges and build dry stone walls. He became curious about how things were made. One day a ropemaker showed him how to weave hammocks, using rope wound around a bobbin. Thomas enjoyed it so much that he made ten!

GOING OUT WITH DAD

Together Thomas and his dad visited Milton Keynes, a new town in south-east England, built by some of the country's top architects. They went to an exhibition about houses of the future. They visited motor shows to see the latest racing cars, and architectural shows to view students' work. Thomas followed his parents' paths: like his father, he was drawn to building and innovation; like his mother, he was interested in materials and craft.

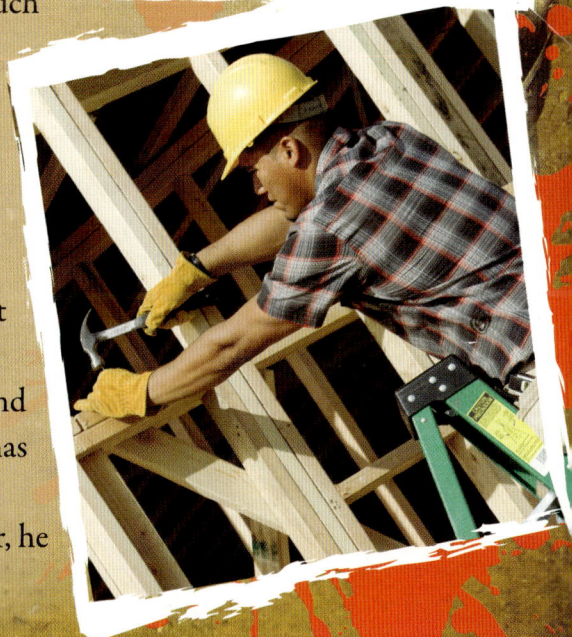

THE YOUNG THOMAS

Looking back, it seems that Thomas was always going to become a designer. He was always drawing and making things. He went to jumble sales and spent his money on old machines such as calculators, typewriters, cameras and clocks. He loved the smell and feel of them. Back home, he took them apart and put them back together again. The bits were spread over his bedroom floor, making it feel like a proper workshop.

In the late 1970s, technology was changing. Out went the old calculating machines, electric typewriters and reel-to-reel tape recorders. In came electronic pocket calculators, word processors and portable cassette players. Thomas could buy the old machines for a few pence.

A CURIOUS CHILD

Thomas had a natural curiosity and liked to follow his interests.

At the age of about ten, he looked round a bus depot and took home some old inner tubes (the squashy tubes you find inside tyres). He turned them into inflatable furniture, then made canvas covers for them that he dyed and sewed himself.

He loved looking at his grandfather's books about Victorian engineers. Every Christmas he was given a book written by the author and illustrator, David Macaulay. These explained in words and pictures how things were made.

A DIFFERENT LIFE

The home and style of living of the Heatherwick family were different from those of other children. Thomas always felt a little bit different but he longed to be the same.

> I'D GO TO MY FRIENDS' HOUSES AND THEY'D HAVE FISH FINGERS, PEAS AND CHIPS – AND THEY WERE WONDERFUL! FOR PACKED LUNCH, I'D COME IN WITH DRIED BANANAS – WHICH LOOK LIKE CAT POO – AND PUMPERNICKEL RYE BREAD. EVERYONE ELSE HAD SLICED BREAD. IT WAS JUST EMBARRASSING.   T.H.

Secondary school had its problems and he changed schools twice. He hated exams and found many of the subjects hard to learn. Nor was he interested in sports: he couldn't see the point of running round a playground, trying to kick a ball. The only things he was good at were drawing and making. This was where he felt strong.

A NICKNAME

Thomas was always interested in ideas. He wanted to know everything there was to know. At school, he was a question machine, always asking teachers, "But how? But why?" He quickly got the nickname "How-Why".

> THERE WERE NO COURSES WHERE YOU STUDIED 'INVENTION': THEY WERE CALLED ARCHITECTURE OR ART OR DESIGN OR COOKING. THE INTERESTING THING FOR ME WAS THE INVENTION, THE PURPOSE. SO I HAD TO WORK OUT THE COURSES, AND WHAT THE WORLD WOULD LET 'INVENTION' BE CALLED.   T.H.

THE NEXT STEP

What should he do when he left school? Thomas wanted to be an inventor, but where do you train to become one? One day his dad took him to visit the Design Centre in London. Part-exhibition and part-shop, it **showcased** modern designs – from fabrics and fridges to teapots and tiles. Thomas saw how design could solve problems and realized this was what he wanted to do.

STUDYING DESIGN

When Thomas left school he did a two-year **diploma** in art and design. He was drawing and making things all the time. Then, at the age of 18, he went on to study at Manchester Polytechnic. He chose his course with care. Although he was very interested in buildings, he didn't choose an architecture course; he was afraid it would be too narrow in focus. He wanted to learn about all kinds of making, so he chose three-dimensional (3D) design instead.

WHAT IS 3D DESIGN?

3D design is about designing and making objects. Everything that has ever been made has been designed by someone somewhere: it might be a multi-storey car park or a small bedside light. How an object looks, feels and works is the result of the designer's skill.

Design has the power to improve or even transform people's lives: whether the object designed is a stand-out building or a smaller item used by people every day. For example, the first a mobile phone with a 'touch' screen was bought by billions of people around the world.

Come and study 3D design

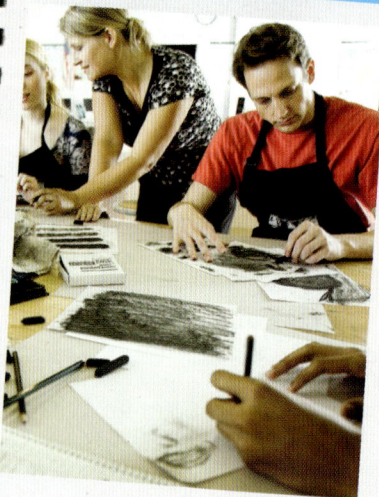

Our 3D design course offers you the chance to:
- explore and study objects
- learn how to represent objects in different ways – as a drawing, a model or a computer design
- develop your practical skills, and make objects from different materials such as glass, ceramic, plastic and wood
- work on small or large **scale** projects, for example in architecture, furniture, model-making and craft.

WHAT'S NEW?

WHEN THOMAS STARTED HIS 3D DESIGN COURSE, THE USE OF COMPUTERS WAS STILL VERY NEW. BEFORE THEN, DESIGNERS' IDEAS WERE DRAWN UP BY SPECIALLY TRAINED **DRAFTSMEN**. TODAY, DESIGNERS WORK ON SCREEN, USING SOFTWARE CALLED COMPUTER-AIDED DESIGN (CAD). THEY CREATE AND IMPROVE THEIR DESIGNS THEMSELVES WITHOUT THE NEED FOR DRAFTSMEN.

A 3D design project for students

Design a bus shelter that meets the following requirements:

* safety for the public
* shelter from the weather
* seating
* information display
* attractive appearance
* strong materials that are easy to maintain
* reasonable cost.

THE RIGHT PLACE

Thomas's years at Manchester Polytechnic were very valuable. At school, he had felt unhappy and uncertain, but here he began to grow more confident.

- He enjoyed working on a wide range of projects, using materials on different scales.
- His tutors were young, open-minded and helpful. They encouraged him rather than taught him.
- He had lots of time to experiment. There was no pressure and no exams.
- He could see the value of the work he was doing. He knew he was in the right place!

11

DESIGN SNAPSHOT:
DESIGN IN THE 1980S AND 1990S

What was happening in the world of 3D design while Thomas was a student? This page shows examples of designs using different scales and materials, ranging from small household goods to landmark architectural designs.

CITRUS FRUIT JUICER, PHILIPPE STARCK, 1990

This orange or lemon juicer is an example of **product design**. It was designed by Frenchman Philippe Starck, and made by an Italian kitchenware company. The design is unusual and it works surprisingly well. It is just the right height to use comfortably and when you press, turn and squeeze the fruit, the juice collects in a glass below. Made out of polished aluminium, it has become a model of good design.

DID YOU KNOW? THE JUICER WAS FIRST SKETCHED ON A PAPER NAPKIN OVER A RESTAURANT LUNCH.

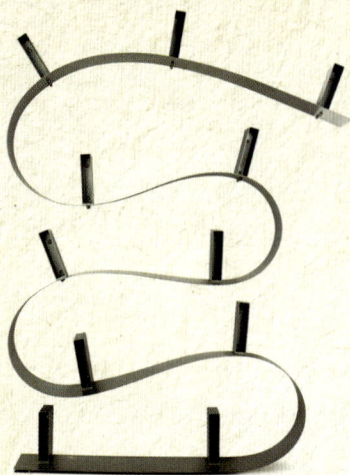

BOOKWORM SHELVING, RON ARAD, 1994

Ron Arad, an Israeli designer, believes that design should not just be useful but surprising and delightful, too. His curvy bookshelf, the Bookworm, takes on different shapes without losing stability or strength. First designed in steel, it was later manufactured in strong, colourful plastic. It is a daring, eye-catching solution for storing books, DVDs and other items.

LOUNGER, MARC NEWSON, 1986

This shiny aluminium lounger looks like something from the future but was based on an antique piece of furniture. The Australian designer, Marc Newson, made his lounger from **fibreglass** and then covered the surface with aluminium sheets. He was a student of sculpture and jewellery design before bringing his skills to product design. This smooth, flowing, metallic chair is like a piece of sculpture.

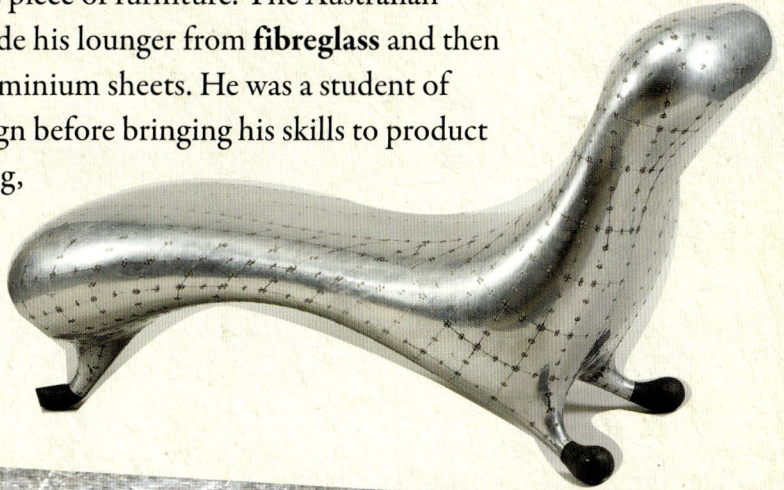

LOUVRE PYRAMID, I.M. PEI, 1989

This large glass and steel pyramid was built in 1989 as an entrance to the Louvre, an art gallery in Paris, France. The Chinese-born American architect believed that the simple transparent shape would blend in well with the historic stone buildings. This mix of old and new was unpopular with some people, but it is now a much-loved landmark of the city.

THINKING BY MAKING

At Manchester, Thomas had a lot of freedom to explore. He had a natural curiosity about materials and all the things you could do with them. He experimented with wire, wood, textiles, plastics, metals, card and rope. He never thought "What can I make with this material?" He simply did what it would allow him to do.

TEST PIECE

Can you match the descriptions of Thomas's test pieces to the pictures opposite?

1) Thomas found some rolls of wire in the materials store at college. He cut off long pieces and spent many hours bending and cutting them with a pair of pliers. He turned them into different shapes.

2) Thomas enjoyed working with textiles. He once used a piece of calico to make a three-dimensional structure. Holding the coarse fabric firmly, he twisted it round in different places, giving it an intriguing appearance.

3) Sometimes Thomas combined rigid and flexible materials. He made a rigid structure out of copper wire. Then he wound rope around the wire frame.

4) Wood fascinated Thomas. He took some thin strips of oak, and then used a stapler to make them into loops of different sizes. He fitted the loops together to produce a form in the shape of a funnel.

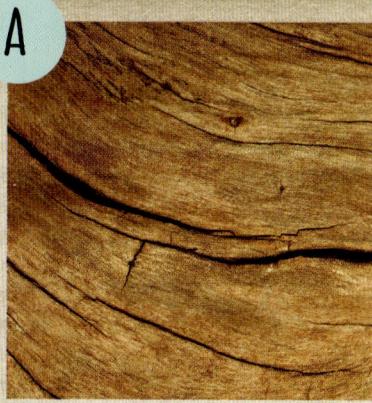

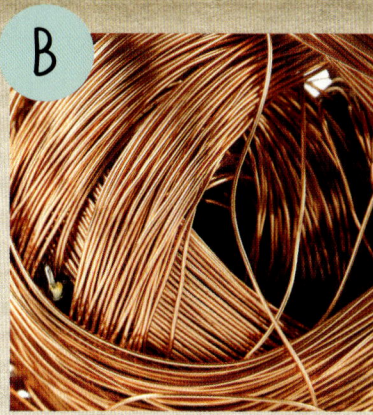

INSPIRING IDEAS

Design is a creative industry. Many designers develop their ideas by drawing or discussing things with others. Thomas found a different route. As he experimented with materials, he found that they offered up lots of useful, unusual ideas.

Working small is easier than working big. When he was working on his test pieces, Thomas had to keep his ideas simple. Yet, deep down, he was always wondering how the ideas and forms he produced might work on a larger scale. Thomas learnt to think by making. This is a special way of working that still inspires him today.

AN ARCHITECTURAL PROJECT BECOMES MATERIAL AT SOME POINT. AT THAT POINT, WHAT ARE YOU GOING TO DO? WHAT MATERIALS ARE YOU GOING TO USE? WHY ARE YOU GOING TO USE THEM? WHY ARE THEY GOING TO MEAN ANYTHING TO ANYONE WHEN YOU DO?   T.H.

BUILDING ON THE PAST

During his first two years at college Thomas worked on small-scale projects, but he always had a strong interest in building. He felt that many new buildings lacked imagination and were uninteresting. He enjoyed the buildings of Brunel and Gaudi but wanted to know, what it was that made them more interesting.

Isambard Kingdom Brunel (1806–1859)
Brunel was a British inventor, designer and engineer who had many different skills. He gave a railway station in London a wonderful steel and glass roof – a new idea at the time.

Antoni Gaudí (1852–1920)
Gaudí was a Spanish architect and builder. He worked closely with metalworkers, potters and other craft experts. His buildings have extraordinary patterns and shapes.

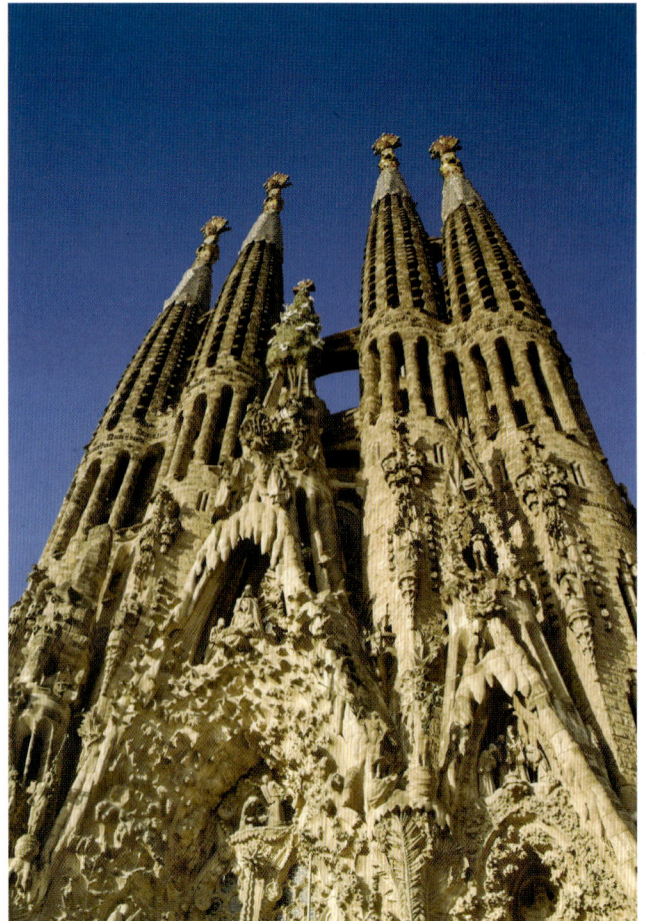

THE MASTER BUILDER

Thomas did a lot of research and believed he found the answer to his question. He explained in his **thesis**:

Back in the 18th and 19th centuries, large building projects were directed by a master builder. This person had many different skills: he was a builder, craftsman, engineer and designer all rolled into one. Of course, he did not do everything himself: he had other engineers, craftsmen and builders to help him. But the shared skills and teamwork meant his designs were always closely linked to how things were made.

By the mid-1800s, this way of working began to change. Architecture and engineering became separate careers and moved away from practical building. So a gap grew between design and making, and this began to make its mark on buildings. Craftsmanship and interesting detail began to disappear.

A NEW CHALLENGE

In his final year at Manchester, Thomas asked to design and make a full-size building – something no student had ever done before. Using the confidence and skills he had gained, he designed a small pavilion suitable for a garden. Of course, other people helped him with it. Thomas believes that, for all the best buildings, designers work in a team. He feels more alive in a team. That was something the pavilion taught him.

> I SPOKE TO MY TUTORS AND SAID, 'I'D LIKE TO MAKE A FULL-SIZE BUILDING, PLEASE'. AND THEY WENT, 'NO, NO, NO, MAKE A MODEL. EVERYONE WILL UNDERSTAND A MODEL.' BUT I KNEW WHAT MY RESEARCH HAD SHOWN. THE REASON I FELT IT WAS SO IMPORTANT THAT THE DESIGNERS OF BUILDINGS MAKE THINGS IS YOU GET A FEELING FOR MATERIALS FROM USING THEM YOURSELF – AND THAT GIVES YOU CONFIDENCE.
>
> T.H.

LAST DAYS AS A STUDENT

After leaving Manchester, Thomas spent two more years as a student of 3D design. He went to London to do a Master's degree at the Royal College of Art (RCA).

He continued to experiment with ways of making buildings. One day, he was making a bench and had two stacks of wooden pieces that he was going to glue together. As he handled them, the stacks tipped and interleaved with one another, rather like a pack of cards. This made an interesting structure, with each stack of wood supporting the other. Would this work in a building?

Thomas used the idea to design a small summerhouse called a gazebo. It was made from hundreds of wooden pieces cut into two simple shapes: one a flat, curved piece; the other a disc. When a famous designer called Sir Terence Conran visited the RCA, Thomas showed him his drawings. Sir Terence liked the design so much that he invited Thomas to build the gazebo in his own garden!

GAZEBO, 1994

Inspiration: Thomas tipped over some piles of plywood pieces and was interested in the way they came to rest.

Unusual features: Made of two stacks of wooden pieces, which pass through and support one another. The walls look solid from close up but transparent from further away.

Key challenge: To make the inside comfortable to lean on when you sit inside the gazebo. The curve in the wooden 'wall' follows the shape of your back.

Site: Thomas built it in the garden of Sir Terence Conran's country house. Then, for his degree show, it was rebuilt outside the RCA.

Materials: Birch plywood.

TERENCE CONRAN

Sir Terence Conran is a British designer. From the 1960s onwards, he produced and sold furniture and other household goods. He is a great supporter of young designers and founded the Design Museum, London, so that everyone can learn about design.

> I TRULY BELIEVE THAT DESIGN MAKES YOU HAPPIER.   T.C.

THE END OF COLLEGE

The gazebo was an important piece in Thomas's final degree show. Degree shows, which are open to the public, display the work of students about to start their careers. Thomas had been studying for seven years. Now he had to take the next step. He decided to set up his own design studio.

GOOD IDEA!

THOMAS CAME UP WITH A CLEVER WAY OF ADVERTISING HIS WORK. HE BOUGHT LOTS OF FLAT WOODEN STICKS - THE ONES DOCTORS USE TO LOOK IN YOUR MOUTH. HE PRINTED THEM WITH HIS NAME AND PHONE NUMBER AND COVERED THEM WITH HOME-MADE ICE CREAM. AT HIS DEGREE SHOW, HE GAVE ONE TO EVERYONE HE MET!

HEATHERWICK STUDIO

In 1994, Thomas set up a small studio in north London with just a handful of people. Business grew and in a few years he moved to the larger space where he works today. Now, over 20 years later, the studio employs more than 160 people.

A DIFFERENT APPROACH

Walk into many design studios, and you will see that they look like offices: designers and architects sit at desks, working quietly at their computers. Heatherwick Studio looks and sounds very different: it has the desks and computers, but it also contains a busy workshop with ten highly-skilled makers. The designers and makers work together and help one another.

> I think this plastic will bend the way I want.

> I think this wood will feel good.

> I think this steel is thick enough to stand up.

WHY HAVE A WORKSHOP?

When a designer starts work on a project, he or she starts to have ideas about what will work, but the designer cannot be absolutely sure an idea works until all the necessary elements are made and tested. That is how the workshop helps: it turns "I think" into "I know".

WHAT THE WORKSHOP DOES

- It tests and proves design ideas.
- It provides the answers to specific questions, such as "How will this handle feel?"
- It allows designers to improve on their ideas and choose the best material.
- It discovers unexpected problems, which it then helps to solve.
- It produces mock-ups, models and prototypes.
- It encourages designers to be inventive.
- It makes the actual, full-scale parts for a project when no one else can.

The workshop uses many different tools, including the latest 3D printers. These create objects by building them up, layer by layer, from powder or plastic. A computer directs the printer nozzle as it sweeps back and forth. With each sweep, it leaves a tiny layer: a precise cross-section of the final object. The finished piece – perhaps a piece of handrail – helps to answer design questions in a matter of hours.

THE LOVELY THING IS POOTLING BETWEEN YOUR COMPUTER AND THE WORKSHOP OR GOING TO CHAT TO SOMEONE WHO KNOWS ALL ABOUT METAL FABRICATION AND THEN COMING BACK AND DRAWING.   STUART WOOD, HEAD OF DESIGN

AT THE CORE, WE ARE MAKERS. WE ARE MAKING PLACES THAT PEOPLE ARE GOING TO LIVE IN AND AROUND. SO THE WHOLE PLACE IS THE WORKSHOP. WE HAVE TO HAVE SOME COMPUTERS IN HERE AND PEOPLE TO WORK THEM, BUT I'M KEEN FOR EVERYONE TO BE REMINDED ALL THE TIME OF OUR RESPONSIBILITY FOR WHAT WE MAKE. AND THE ONLY WAY IS TO BE NEAR TO THE MAKING.   T.H.

WHO WORKS AT HEATHERWICK STUDIO?

Heatherwick Studio employs a mix of people from many different backgrounds. There are architects, engineers and product designers. There are experts on computers and digital technology. There are people who have trained as artists, and have worked in sculpture, metalwork or jewellery design.

Some people now work in different areas from the ones in which they trained: a product designer works on buildings; a **fine artist** runs the workshop; a ballet student works as a technician. The overlap of art, science and design helps the studio to come up with exciting and original ideas.

WHO DOES WHAT?

JOB TITLE: HEAD OF INNOVATION

Job description: to work on ground-breaking projects; to find new ways of doing things
Training: four years studying product design

JOB TITLE: ARCHITECT

Job description: to work on architectural projects, from design to construction
Training: seven years studying architecture plus two years of practical experience

JOB TITLE: HEAD OF MAKING

Job description: to manage the workshop; to make mock-ups, models and prototypes; to assist designers in solving problems
Training: seven years at art school, studying sculpture

JOB TITLE: DESIGNER

Job description: to work on a variety of projects, at every level and at every scale; to lead the design of large-scale projects; to develop ideas for competitions

Training: five years' architecture training plus two years of practical experience

JOB TITLE: HEAD OF INFORMATION TECHNOLOGY

Job description: to make sure the studio's technology – computers, 3D printers, laser cutters, etc. – functions properly

Training: four years studying computer sciences

JOB TITLE: PRESS OFFICER

Job description: to deal with enquiries from the **press** and other media; to generate publicity for the studio and provide information about it

Training: three years studying Art History

JOB TITLE: MODEL MAKER

Job description: to make 3D models from design drawings

Training: three years studying for a model-making degree

A TEAM EFFORT

People are put into teams to work on different projects. Thomas works with all the teams and encourages them to use their skills to get results. It's not the way design is taught in schools. There, pupils usually work alone and carry the responsibility for a project. In the studio no one carries this burden: design is a team effort.

SITTING BY MYSELF TRYING TO BE BRILLIANT WASN'T A GREAT THING. IT WAS WHEN I WORKED WITH OTHERS THAT IT ALL CAME ALIVE. THE TEAMS PROVOKE ME - WE PROVOKE EACH OTHER - AND WE DO WONDERFUL THINGS BETWEEN US.   T.H.

A NEW PROJECT

A new project takes time and has its ups and downs.

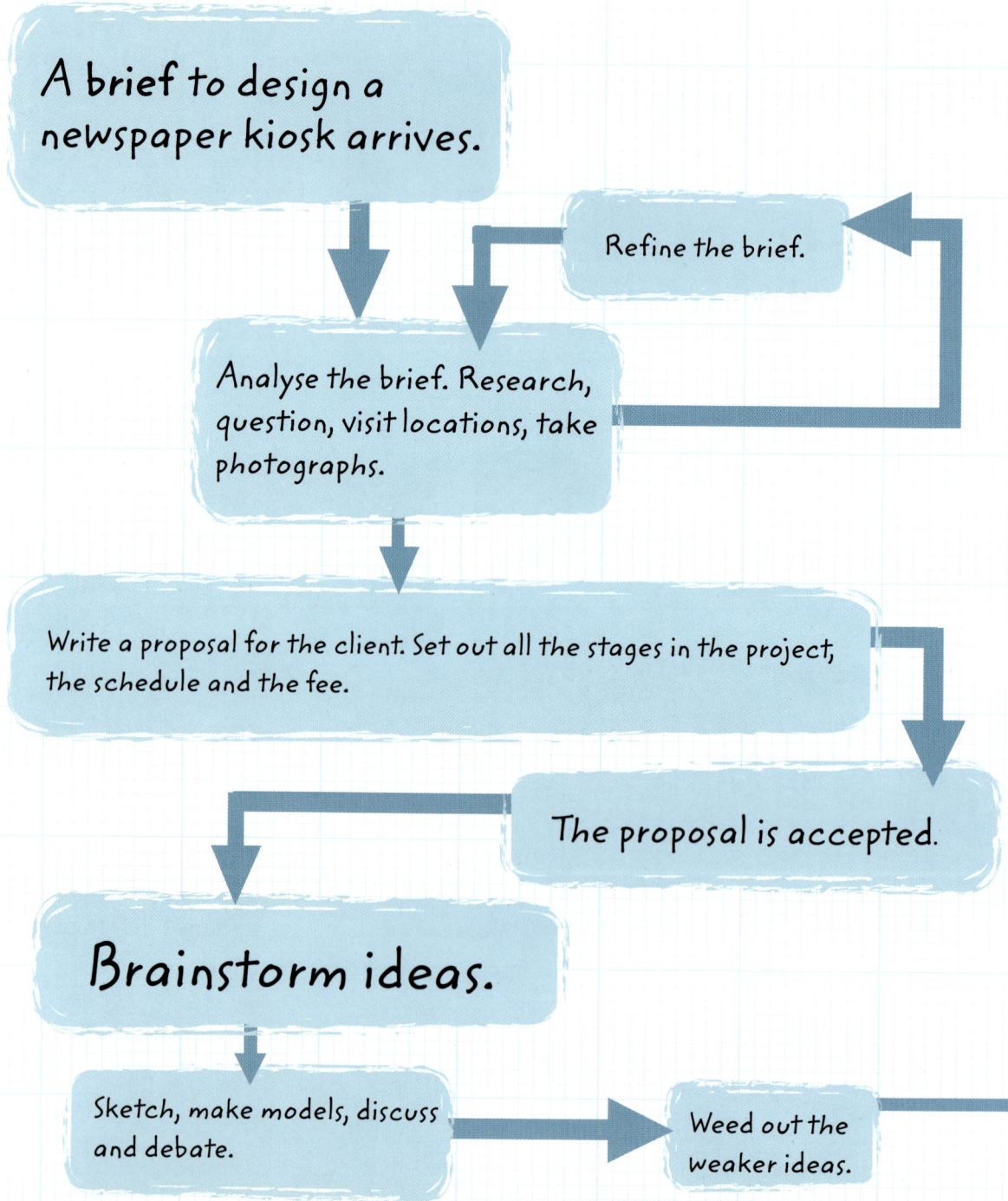

A brief to design a newspaper kiosk arrives.

Refine the brief.

Analyse the brief. Research, question, visit locations, take photographs.

Write a proposal for the client. Set out all the stages in the project, the schedule and the fee.

The proposal is accepted.

Brainstorm ideas.

Sketch, make models, discuss and debate.

Weed out the weaker ideas.

Show the client the ideas. Decide on your favourites together.

Look at possible materials. Agree on the best ones.

Develop the designs in detail. The workshop makes a prototype shelf for the kiosk.

The prototype doesnt quite work. Refine the design and make another prototype.

Narrow the remaning designs down to two. Make a model of your favourite.

Present the model to the client. They like it but it will be expensive.

Cut costs and complete the design.

The client approves the final design.

IT'S A SCARY PROCESS, THERE ARE SO MANY UNKNOWNS AND IT DOESN'T MEAN IT'S ALWAYS ALL RIGHT IN THE END. YOU HAVE TO BE ON YOUR TOES ALL THE TIME TO TRY TO MAKE THE MOST OF THE POSSIBILITIES THAT A PROJECT CAN OFFER. THAT'S WHAT WE FEEL OUR JOB IS TO TRY TO DO.   T.H.

THOMAS MAKES A SPLASH

One of the first projects to make Thomas's name was his design for the shop windows of Harvey Nichols, a luxury department store in London.

LOCATION:	Harvey Nichols, Knightsbridge, London
BRIEF:	To design a display for 12 shop windows that will put the store in the spotlight during London Fashion Week 1997
ISSUES TO CONSIDER:	Harvey Nichols has a reputation for its exciting window displays. We are looking for creative, traffic-stopping design.

DAILY NEWS
September 1997

Young designer wows London with 'intruding' windows

Gifted young designer, Thomas Heatherwick, 27, has won a top design award for his window display at fashionable Harvey Nichols. Heatherwick calls his work 'Autumn intrusion'. It is a 200 metre long structure that wriggles in and out of the 12 windows – like an intruder breaking in and out of the store.

Carved by hand

The extraordinary sculpture was designed by hand. Heatherwick carved a model out of polystyrene with a kitchen knife. The finished sculpture is made of many sections. Each section was scaled up, drawn onto large sheets of graph paper, and carved out of blocks of polystyrene. Finally, it was covered with ultra-thin plywood. The project took a team six months to build and ten nights to put up.

AUTUMN INTRUSION, 1997

Inspiration: I wanted the window display to connect with the architecture of the whole building.

Unusual features: It's a wriggling wooden sculpture that weaves in and out of the shop windows all along the street.

Key challenge: It had to be strong enough to stand up to the wind but light enough to build and hang.

Materials: Carved blocks of strong polystyrene covered with thin birch plywood.

PUBLIC REACTION

Thomas's windows got a huge reaction. The shop, the public and the newspapers loved it. It won Thomas his first big award. Heatherwick Studio had arrived!

DID YOU KNOW?
FOR HIS SCULPTURE, THOMAS COPIED THE HUMAN BONE: IT WAS STRONG ON THE OUTSIDE AND LIGHT IN THE MIDDLE.

ORIGAMI TOWERS

Near St Paul's Cathedral in London is an open space called Paternoster Square. Hidden from view, beneath the Square, is an electricity **substation**, which distributes electricity to the city. In 2000, it needed a new cooling system and Heatherwick Studio was asked to design it. It was a simple, mechanical, functional request – the kind that Thomas likes best!

THE BRIEF

LOCATION:	Paternoster Square, London
BRIEF:	To design a cooling tower for an underground electricity substation
ISSUES TO CONSIDER:	• The cooling tower needs to house two large air vents: one to draw cool air into the station; the other to carry warm air out. • The site is next to St Paul's Cathedral. The design needs to fit in with this historic monument.

THE SIZE PROBLEM

Thomas and his team met the **commissioners** to discuss the brief. The commissioners wanted to hide the cooling system inside a large tower. Thomas and his team felt a bulky tower would look out of place and dominate the square.

FINDING A SOLUTION

With the project engineers, the design team discussed ways of reducing the tower. They discovered that they could do it! The cool air didn't need a vent: it could be drawn into the substation through metal grilles set into the pavement. The vent that carried warm air out could be split into two. So instead of having one massive tower, there could be two slimmer structures with a pathway inbetween.

FROM PAPER TO STEEL

The team began to think about what form the structures might have. One day, on a shelf in the studio, they noticed a twisting paper structure that looked like **origami**. It was a test piece from Thomas's student days. The design team realized the twisting form might be right for the vents. Engineers made the calculations and it all worked out! The twisting vents were made of stainless steel and looked like beautiful sculptures.

The towers are not identical but mirror images of each other.

Each tower is made from 63 triangles, cut from eight millimetre thick stainless steel plate, welded together.

The triangles are set at angles to each other. They reflect the light in different ways and appear to be made from different materials.

They stand 11 metres high – as tall as a three-storey building.

GOOD IDEA!

THOMAS WANTED THE STAINLESS STEEL TO HAVE A SOFT, SILKY FINISH. INSTEAD OF BLASTING IT WITH SAND, WHICH GIVES STEEL A ROUGH FINISH, HE BLASTED IT WITH TINY GLASS BEADS. THIS PROCESS IS COMMONLY USED ON JEWELLERY AND OTHER SMALL-SCALE ITEMS.

THE ZIP BAG

As well as working for clients, the designers at Heatherwick Studio sometimes develop ideas of their own.

Experimenting with materials was always a fruitful source of ideas for Thomas. One day, he discovered that it was possible to buy a roll of zip that was 200 metres long. He began to wonder about it. A zip is usually just an extra – something that is used to make an opening. Could an extra-long zip become the main material for another product?

CREATING A BESTSELLER

Thomas and his team began to experiment with the long zips. They made lamp shades out of zips, a dress out of a zip and many different bags out of zips.

The bag seemed to be the most interesting and practical idea. The studio showed it to a French company that sold luxury leather products. They were extremely enthisiastic! Together Heatherwick Studio and the French company perfected the bag and brought it out in a range of colours. It became one of their bestselling items.

ASK AN ENGINEER

There was a niggling problem with the bag. When the long zip was sewn into spirals, it twisted badly and wouldn't sit straight. An engineer had a look at it. He had worked on a lot of buildings but had never made a handbag before. After several months of tricky calculations, he worked out how to make the bag in a way that stopped it twisting.

A SINGLE LONG PIECE OF ZIP.

STRIPS OF FABRIC INBETWEEN THE ZIP.

WHEN YOU OPEN THE ZIP, THE BAG DOUBLES IN SIZE. IT ALSO REVEALS A SPIRAL OF COLOUR.

RESULT!

The French company was so impressed by Heatherwick Studio that it asked the studio to design its new shop in New York.

WHAT'S NEW?

THE MODERN ZIP FIRST APPEARED ABOUT 100 YEARS AGO. BEFORE THEN, SHIRTS, SKIRTS, BOOTS AND BAGS OPENED AND CLOSED WITH HOOKS AND BUTTONS, WHICH TOOK A LOT OF TIME AND EFFORT. INVENTING THE ZIP WAS NOT STRAIGHTFORWARD: IT TOOK SEVERAL ENGINEERS 20 YEARS TO PERFECT. THE ZIP BAG CELEBRATES A CLEVER DEVICE THAT CONTAINS A HUGE AMOUNT OF DESIGN.

DESIGN SNAPSHOT: BAGS

How do you wear a bag: on your arm, on your back or around your waist? How do you use it? For some, a bag is just a useful tool to carry shopping or other belongings; for others, it's a beautiful **accessory**, like a piece of jewellery. All the bags on this page are stand-out designs.

BUM BAG, 1996

The French firm, Louis Vuitton, has been making bags and luggage for 150 years. In 1896, they designed their famous waterproof canvas, decorated with 'LV', the company's initials. In 1996, a fashion designer called Vivienne Westwood celebrated the material's 100th anniversary by using it to design a bum bag! When a woman wears it, the bag looks rather like a bustle – the pad that filled out women's skirts in the 19th century.

BIRKIN BAG, 1981

The French company Hermès named its famous bag after an English actress. Selling for the price of a small car, each bag is made out of expensive materials. The outside is made of calf, ostrich, crocodile or lizard leather; there is a goatskin lining; and the clasps are plated with gleaming gold. Each bag is handmade by an expertly-trained craftsman or craftswoman. The end result is not just a bag: it's a symbol of wealth and status.

"I'M NOT A PLASTIC BAG", 2005

When this simple cotton bag went on sale it sold out in just a few hours. Such is the power of design. The bag was created by designer, Anya Hindmarch, whose luxury leather bags sell for high prices. This bag was designed to encourage people to stop using plastic bags, which are bad for the environment. It had an enviromental message, but also became a fashion statement.

MESSENGER BAG, 1989

This bag represents the freewheeling lifestyle of its young designer, Rob Honeycutt. He was working as a bike messenger in San Francisco when he designed his first bags. The bags became popular during the Internet boom, when many young people cycled to work carrying a laptop computer. Rob encouraged his customers to design their own bags, using his website. These one-of-a-kind, repairable products are still made in San Francisco, by people who cycle to work!

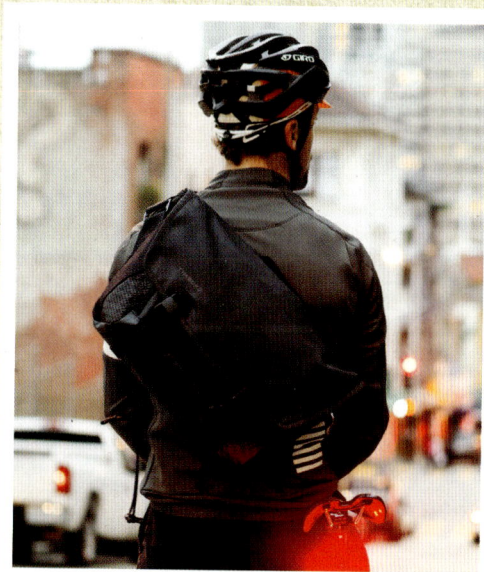

CHRISTMAS CARDS

Thomas Heatherwick grew up around people who didn't buy cards to send at Christmas: they made them by hand instead. So Thomas made his own cards, too.

WORKS OF ART

From the earliest days at the studio, Thomas decided to send cards to everyone who had helped him get started. Each year's card was a work of art, and was produced in the studio workshop. The project team worked closely with their local post office to make sure that these special cards could be sent through the mail.

> IT WAS THE WAY I NEEDED TO SHOW APPRECIATION. TO GIVE SOMEONE YOUR TIME AND IDEAS SEEMED THE BEST THING TO DO. AND IT WASN'T ABOUT MONEY. T.H.

WHICH IS WHICH?

The five cards on this page were sent to Thomas's family, friends and supporters - a different card each Christmas. Can you match the descriptions of each card to its picture?

A
In 1997, it cost 21 pence to send a card by post. Thomas stuck 21 one-penny stamps on a card in the shape of a Christmas tree. He put the address at the bottom, as if it were the pot of a tree. The round postmarks on the stamps look like baubles on the tree.

B
This card is a small wooden box. It has a transparent front and four stamps inside. The name and address are on the back of the box along with a small cord with a star. When you pull on the cord, the stamps fold back using tiny wires up to reveal the Christmas message.

C

This card looks like a charm bracelet. Two-penny stamps and their postmarks have been cut out and linked to make a chain. Each card comes with a label with the name, address and message.

D

This card is formed using four white envelopes, lined with green tissue paper. When you open the first envelope, you find a smaller one inside — and so on, until you reach the fourth envelope and find a chocolate Father Christmas. The whole thing hangs together with ribbon and looks like a Christmas tree.

E

This card looks like a pine cone. It is made of 25 one-penny stamps stuck to each other. It has been dipped in transparent resin to make it strong enough to send through the post. Each 'cone' has a label with the name, address and message.

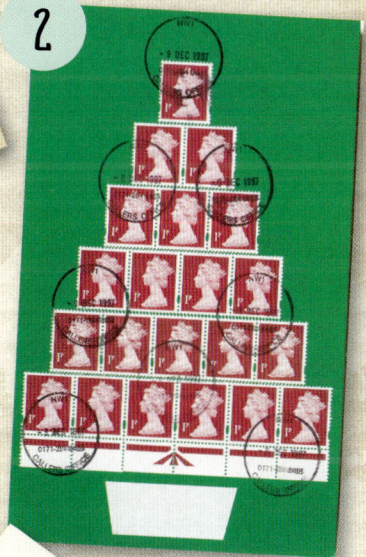

A MAGIC BRIDGE

Every Friday lunchtime in west London, a small crowd gathers beside a bridge over a canal. Silently the bridge begins to move. It lifts itself up off the ground, curves upwards and curls into a ball. The audience cheers and claps. This is the rolling bridge; it is one of Heatherwick Studio's most popular designs.

THE BRIEF

LOCATION:	Paddington Basin, west London: a big development of houses, shops and offices near a junction of two canals.
BRIEF:	To design a pedestrian bridge across a narrow canal.
ISSUES TO CONSIDER:	• The bridge will provide a route for people who live or work in the development. • It has to be possible to open the bridge to let boats through.

HOW IT WORKS

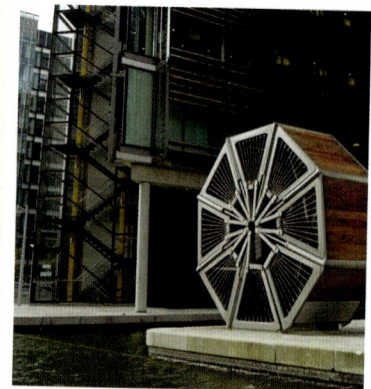

1 The bridge is plain and simple. Most of the time, it is down.

2 Inside the seven pairs of posts are powerful **hydraulic rams**. At the push of a button, the rams lengthen. They push on the handrails, making them fold.

3 The walkway is made of eight hinged sections. They fold in on themselves, and make the bridge curl up.

HOW DO BRIDGES MOVE?

Bridges can open in many different ways. For example, they can:

* tilt up
* 'break' in two
* swing round
* fold up.

Thomas and his team rejected these options for their new bridge. They wanted it to transform itself, in a way that was both surprising and graceful. Working closely with engineers and welders, they produced the rolling bridge. It is a marriage of art, science and engineering and has won a number of awards. At present, the rolling bridge is the only bridge of its type in existence.

ROLLING BRIDGE, 2002

Inspiration: one of the dinosaurs in the film *Jurassic Park*. It had a long tail that moved very fluidly. Thomas wanted something like this for the bridge.
Unusual features: the bridge curls up into a ball.
Key challenge: to find a way of moving the bridge away from the canal.
Site: Paddington Basin, west London.
Materials: steel, stainless steel cables, timber walkway, aluminium treads. All the materials are very plain and blend into the background.

WHAT'S NEW?

THOMAS HAS AN IDEA FOR ANOTHER NEW BRIDGE. IT WOULD BE MADE OF 1200 GLASS PIECES, WHICH ARE SQUEEZED SO TIGHTLY TOGETHER THAT THEY FORM A STRONG WALKWAY. PERHAPS, ONE DAY, THE GLASS BRIDGE WILL BE BUILT AND YOU WILL WALK ACROSS IT!

DESIGN SNAPSHOT: BRIDGES

Bridges span rivers, roads, lakes and canals. They carry road vehicles, trains, pedestrians and cyclists. Each bridge has a unique location and requires a unique solution. Architects and engineers work closely together. They try to come up with a bridge design in which the function, appearance and experience of using it are all closely linked.

MILLAU VIADUCT

What is it? A 2500-metre-long **viaduct**. It carries a motorway over a wide river valley.

Where is it? Near Millau, south–west France.

When was it opened? 2004, exactly three years after building began.

Designer: French engineer, Michel Virlogeux and British architect Norman Foster.

Materials: Steel and concrete.

Why is it special? It is the highest bridge in the world.

Did you know? The tallest mast measures 343 metres – ten metres higher than the Eiffel Tower.

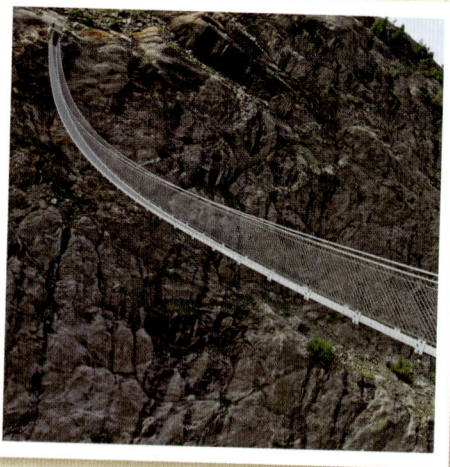

TRAVERSINA FOOTBRIDGE

What is it? A 56-metre-long pedestrian bridge. It carries a hiking trail across a steep gorge.

Where is it? Near Zillis in Switzerland.

Designer: Swiss engineer and architect, Jürg Conzett.

When was it built? 2005.

Materials: Steel and timber.

Why is it special? The bridge is like a staircase, and is 22 metres steeper at one end than it is at the other. This is because the hiking trails are at different levels.

Did you know? The bridge's cables and walkway were assembled in mid-air using a helicopter.

MOSES BRIDGE

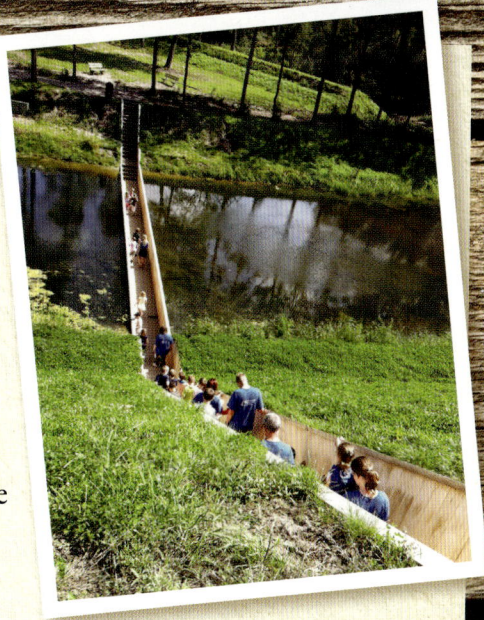

What is it? A pedestrian bridge that crosses a moat to an old fortress.

Where is it? Halsteren, the Netherlands.

Designer: An architectural company called RO&AD.

When was it opened? 2011.

Materials: A waterproofed hardwood called accoya.

Why is it special? A moat was a line of defence so the designers felt it would be wrong to build a bridge over the top. Their bridge is a trench, sunk into the water. From a distance it is invisible and so preserves the feel of the ancient moat.

Did you know? The bridge is named after Moses, a prophet in the Bible who parted the waters of the Red Sea.

HENDERSON WAVE BRIDGE

What is it? A 274-metre-long pedestrian bridge that crosses a six-lane highway. It forms part of an outdoor trail linking two national parks.

Where is it? Singapore.

Designer: Liu Thai-Ker, an architect–planner from Singapore.

When was it opened? 2008.

Materials: A steel structure with a wooden walkway.

Why is it special? It has a beautiful wave-like structure. The timber walkway carries you through the top of a forest, where you can see animals and plants.

Did you know? At night, the bridge is lit up and looks like a long snake.

A WINNING PAVILION

In 2010, an international fair called the World Expo was held in Shanghai, China. Heatherwick Studio won the competition to design a special pavilion to promote the UK.

LOOKING FOR A THEME

THE BRIEF

LOCATION:	Shanghai, China
BRIEF:	To design the UK pavilion for Expo 2010
ISSUES TO CONSIDER:	• The theme of the fair is 'Better cities, better life'. • The pavilion should show the UK in a strong light. • The pavilion should be in the top five in the final competition.

Thomas and his team discussed the theme 'Better cities, better life'. They knew that London was the world's greenest city, thanks to its many parks and gardens. They also knew that gardens and plants were important to the UK as a whole. They became interested in the Millennium Seed Bank, where UK scientists were storing the seeds of hundreds of thousands of the world's plants. The team began to think about seeds: they look dry and humble but, as they grow into plants, they provide us with medicines, food and beauty. They are one of the world's treasures.

A CATHEDRAL TO SEEDS

So the team designed a Seed Cathedral. The structure was just a simple plywood box but the walls were pierced by 60 000 long transparent rods. They extended inside and outside the building, and had seeds displayed at their tips. The rods, which looked like hairs, bent and waved in the breeze, just like a field of grasses. They gave the pavilion an extraordinary texture.

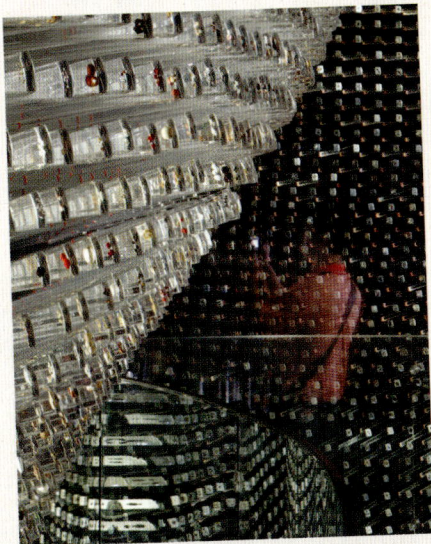

DAILY NEWS

'Hairy' building wins Expo's top prize

At a ceremony in Shanghai last night, the UK pavilion, designed by Heatherwick Studio, beat 240 others to win the Gold Medal for pavilion design.

The building has been the star attraction of this year's fair. However, the story does not end here. When the building is taken down, the 250 000 seeds displayed in its 'hairs' will be given to students in China and the UK. The plan is to educate them about the importance of plants.

The Pavilion has brought the work of Heatherwick Studio to a wider audience and has helped it win more work in Asia.

> PEOPLE QUEUED AND FOUGHT TO GET IN AND IT WAS THRILLING. EIGHT MILLION PEOPLE WENT TO SEE IT. IT WAS GREAT TO HAVE A HIT ON OUR HANDS.   T.H.

DESIGN SNAPSHOT: EXPO PAVILIONS

The sensational buildings designed for World Expos do not have a long life. Most of them, like Thomas's Seed Cathedral, are demolished soon after the event. However, some pavilions from the past have managed to survive and become famous, and can be visited today.

THE EIFFEL TOWER

What is it? A-324-metre high tower with restaurants and viewing platforms.
Where is it? Paris, France.
When was it built? 1889.
Designer: Gustave Eiffel, a French engineer.
Materials: Wrought iron.
What's the idea? The tower celebrated French engineering, industry and science.
Legacy: It has been visited by over 260 million people and is one of the most recognisable buildings in the world today.
Did you know? The first visitors to the tower had to walk up to the viewing platforms as the lifts had not been completed.

THE ATOMIUM

What is it? Half-sculpture and half-architecture, the Atomium represents an iron **molecule** magnified 165 billion times. The nine spheres represent the atoms inside the molecule.
Where is it? Brussels, Belgium.
When was it built? 1958.
Designer: André Waterkeyn, a Belgian engineer.
Materials: Aluminium and steel.
What's the idea? The structure was a celebration of scientific and human progress.
Legacy: Now a museum, the Atomium is a popular tourist attraction and a symbol of Belgium.
Did you know? In 2004, the dull aluminium 'skin' was replaced with shiny stainless steel plates.

THE BARCELONA PAVILION

What is it? A sleek modern house made of beautiful materials.

Where is it? Barcelona, Spain.

When was it built? 1929.

Designer: Ludwig Mies van der Rohe, a German–American architect.

Materials: Steel, glass and marble.

What's the idea? Built as Germany's pavilion for the World Fair, it celebrated new ideas in building.

Legacy: It is a world-class piece of architecture and still inspires architects today.

Did you know? The pavilion was demolished in 1930 but was re-built on the same site in 1986.

THE SPACE NEEDLE

What is it? A 184-metre-high tower with a 'flying saucer' at the top. This contains a revolving restaurant and observation deck.

Where is it? Seattle, Washington, USA.

When was it built? 1962.

Designer: Edward Carlson, John Graham and Victor Steinbrueck.

Materials: Steel and concrete.

What's the idea? The tower celebrated the Space Age and looked to the future.

Legacy: The Space Needle is a symbol of Seattle and a world-famous landmark.

Did you know? The Space Needle sways in the wind. It moves about 16 millimetres for every ten kilometres per hour of wind.

ALL ABOARD! A NEW BUS FOR LONDON

The team at Heatherwick Studio was excited to be asked to design a new London bus. Public transport is very important in cities and a bus is something that everyone can use and, if well-designed, enjoy!

THE BRIEF

LOCATION:	London
BRIEF:	To design a London bus for the 21st century

ISSUES TO CONSIDER:	• The new bus should use 40 per cent less fuel than existing buses.
	• To reduce stopping time, it should have:
	    • three doors
	    • two staircases
	    • an open rear platform.
	• It should be:
	    • accessible to wheelchair users
	    • easy for people with prams
	    • affordable
	    • red.

BUS TIMELINE

JULY 2008
A competition to design a new London bus is announced.

MAY 2010
Their design is put on display.

NOVEMBER 2010
A full-size mock-up is built so users can test the bus. The **feedback** helps to improve the design.

JANUARY 2010
Heatherwick Studio is invited to do the final design.

MAY 2011
A working vehicle is built and tested. It travels nearly 10 000 km.

IMPROVEMENTS

The new buses are quiet and clean because they use the latest green technology. They run on two kinds of power: a battery-powered electric motor and a diesel-run generator that charges the batteries when they need topping up.

- Three sets of doors make it easier and quicker to get on and off.

- Two staircases provide easy access to and from the upper deck.

- Stairs, handrails, lighting and bell buttons all have the same simple colours.

- A lightweight aluminium body makes the bus more fuel-efficient.

- There is a large hop-on, hop-off platform for daytime use.

- The rear door is driver-operated and closes at night.

- The low floor helps wheelchair users. It drops a further 7 cm when the bus comes to a stop.

- Small lights give a soft, warm glow.

- Large windows give a light, airy feel.

- Rounded corners and edges make the bus look smaller.

NOVEMBER 2011 The first bus rolls off the production line.

TRAVELLING ROUND LONDON IN A CONVERTIBLE SPORTS CAR IS THE WORST WAY TO SEE THE CITY. THE BEST IS FROM THE UPSTAIRS OF A BUS. YOU GET THE BIGGER VIEW.   T.H.

FEBRUARY 2012
The first buses appear on the streets.

BY 2016
More than 600 new buses will be in operation.

DESIGN SNAPSHOT: TRANSPORT

These pages look at ground-breaking transport designs – from motorbikes to mountain bikes and from high-speed trains to supersonic aircraft. Each one meets a different need: to be fast, cheap or environmentally friendly.

VESPA

In the mid-1940s, motorcycles were bulky, uncomfortable and dirty. The new 'Vespa' scooter changed all that. Designed by an Italian aircraft engineer, it had many great features: an easy step-through frame; a safe, comfortable riding position; and a front panel to protect the rider from dirt. Manufactured just after the Second World War, the Vespa gave Italians a cheap form of transport that is still popular across Europe. It has become a symbol of Italian style.

Did you know?

Vespa is the Italian word for 'wasp'. The scooter's shape resembled a wasp and its small engine made a buzzing sound.

MAGLEV TRAIN

Maglev trains are high-speed trains that run in Japan and China. They have no wheels and do not run on tracks. Instead, they have powerful magnets to lift the train and pull it forwards. Because it hovers above the track, the train gives a smoother ride and is unaffected by bad weather. The latest trains (which are due in 2027) will travel at speeds of up to 500 kilometres per hour.

Did you know?

The word 'maglev' is short for magnetic levitation.

CONCORDE

Concorde (1976–2003) was a supersonic passenger aircraft, built by French and British engineers. It regularly reached speeds of 2160 kilometres per hour – which is twice the speed of sound – and could fly from London to New York in roughly three hours. Built mostly from aluminium, the plane had a long, needle-shaped nose and slender swept-back wings. People nicknamed the aircraft Big Bird, and admired it for its beauty as much as for its speed.

Did you know?
Concorde's long nose tilted down before landing so that the pilot could see the runway.

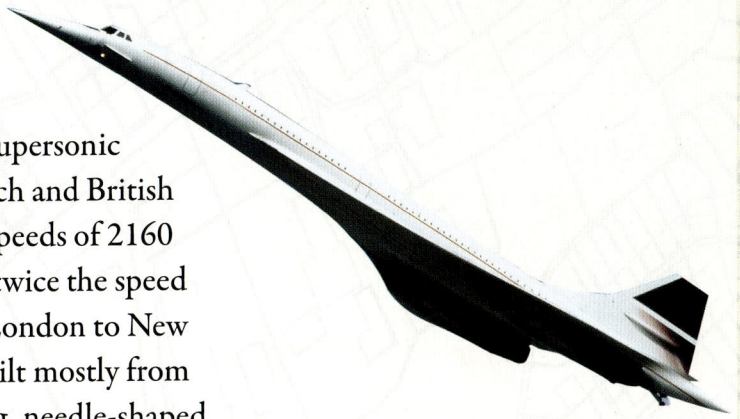

MOUNTAIN BIKE

The mountain bike first appeared in the early 1980s. The new bike could be ridden off-road, over rough **terrain**. Its design was different from a normal bike: it had an extra-strong frame; a **suspension system** to improve the ride; wider tyres with plenty of tread; wide, straight handlebars for better control; and extra gears for hill-climbing. Mountain bikes were a huge success: they started a new sport and allowed people in towns and cities to get out and have an adventure.

Did you know?
The pioneers of mountain-biking adapted normal road bikes for their off-road fun. These could only be ridden downhill!

DESIGNING A MOMENT: THE OLYMPIC CAULDRON

In 2011, Heatherwick Studio was asked to design the cauldron that would hold the Olympic flame during the 2012 Games. This was a big responsibility: lighting the cauldron was an important moment during the opening ceremony. It would be seen by millions of people all around the world.

> OUR ROLE WAS TO DESIGN A MOMENT: HOW COULD WE MAKE THIS MOMENT? WE DIDN'T JUST WANT TO MAKE A BOWL ON A STICK. T.H.

A SYMBOL FOR THE GAMES

Thomas and his team spent two months thinking about the cauldron. They wanted it to be 'made' at the ceremony itself. They decided that each country would bring a gift into the stadium – a gleaming copper element. Each element would contain a small burner and connect to a circle of rods in the stadium. When the moment came and the burners were lit, the elements would rise, creating the cauldron and a huge flame. It would be a symbol of the unity of the Games.

A COMPLEX DEVICE

The studio drew the designs. The cauldron was a complex device with hundreds of moving parts: pivots, levers, gas pipes, burners, lighting systems, and so on. The designs were sent to a workshop that made large one-off projects. The workshop managed to build the cauldron, using a combination of the latest computer technology and traditional craft skills.

ELEMENT FACTS

- Copper was chosen because it is a warm colour and strong heat gives it an interesting, rainbow-like coating.
- Each element was unique: it had its own delicate shape and was engraved with the name of a country.
- The form of each element was first made in wood before a thin sheet of copper was hand-beaten around it. The people who did this usually worked on vintage car repairs.
- Over 600 elements were made for three different cauldrons: one set for the Olympics, one set for the Paralympics and one set for rehearsals and testing.
- After the Games, each nation took home its own element as a souvenir.

TESTING, TESTING

The studio and the workshop worked on the cauldron for nine months. Every part was carefully tested: the way the rods rose and fell, the way the elements locked together, the way the flames lit and burned. In June 2012, the cauldron was moved to the Olympic stadium. During a rehearsal the night before the Games, one of the rods on the cauldron jammed. The team managed to fix the problem and never told Thomas about it. Fortunately it was all right on the night!

'BETTY' IN NUMBERS

HEIGHT: 8.5 METRES
WIDTH: 18 METRES WHEN FLAT ON THE GROUND
STRUCTURE: 204 RODS IN 10 RINGS, ATTACHED TO A 5-STEP BASE
WEIGHT: 32 TONNES
LIFTING TIME: 40 SECONDS

TOP SECRET

The Olympic cauldron was so secret that it had a codename, 'Betty' (after a team member's dog). All the testing at the workshop took place behind tall screens. Testing at the stadium took place in the middle of the night when there was a no-fly zone over the stadium. No one could spy on 'Betty' from the air and leak the story.

LOOKING TO THE FUTURE

Today, Heatherwick Studio is over 20 years old. It has grown from a small group of people into a large organization. It is working on exciting projects in the UK, USA, China, Singapore, South Africa and the Middle East.

PROJECTS AROUND THE WORLD

New project 1: Public park, Abu Dhabi, United Arab Emirates

This new park, for a city in the desert, contains gardens, pools, cafés and a library. It has a 20-metre-high canopy, to protect the people and plants from the hot sun. The canopy is shaped to look like the dry desert landscape.

New project 2: Art gallery, Cape Town, South Africa

The new gallery will stand in an old **silo**. The huge concrete chambers, where grain was once stored, have been carved out to make galleries. New windows bulge out from the outside walls.

New project 3: University building, Singapore

The building is a cluster of towers built around a large central space. They contain 56 classrooms and have gardens on some of the floors.

A NEW BRIDGE

A current Heatherwick Studio project in the UK is the Garden Bridge.

Q: What is the Garden Bridge?

A: It is a new public garden, which will be planted on a bridge over the river Thames, London. The 370-metre-long garden bridge will be the first of its kind in the world.

Q: How is it different from other bridges?

A: Most bridges are just crossing points. This one will be planted with grasses, wild flowers, bushes and trees. The bridge will be a place to sit and stroll, with great views of the river and the city.

Q: Why build it?

A: The bridge will improve links for pedestrians between the north and south banks of the river Thames. It will also be a major new tourist attraction.

Q: When will building start?

A: The studio hopes that work will start in 2015 and that the bridge will open in late 2018.

IT'S TAKEN A LONG TIME TO BE DOING WHAT I WROTE AS A STUDENT 20 YEARS AGO. IT TAKES A LONG TIME TO BE TRUSTED TO WORK ON BIG NATIONAL PROJECTS. AT THE MOMENT WE'RE BUILDING OUR FIRST BUILDING THAT IS BIGGER THAN A SINGLE STOREY. SO IT TAKES TIME. SO I FEEL I'M JUST BEGINNING.   T.H.

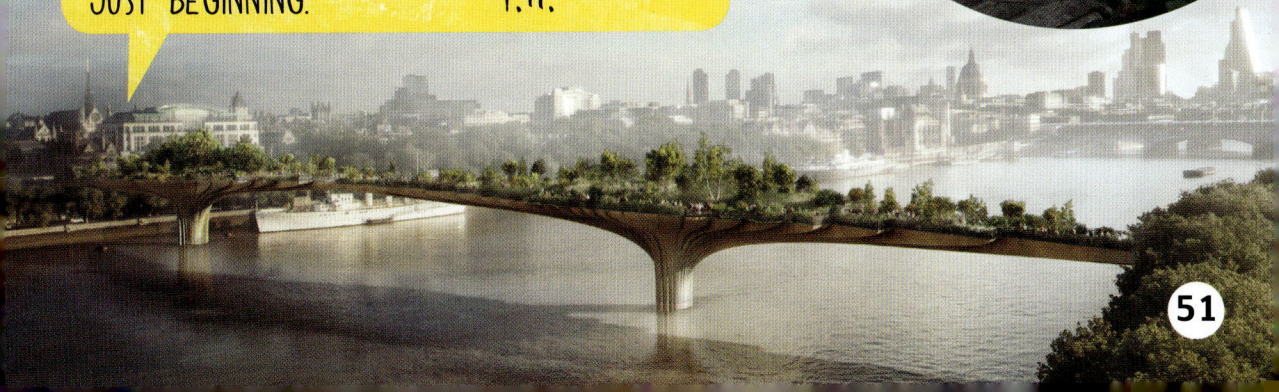

THE STORY SO FAR: A TIMELINE

1970 Thomas Heatherwick born in London

1988 Attends Manchester Polytechnic to study 3D design

1991 Designs the pavilion
Graduates from Manchester Polytechnic

1992 Attends the Royal College of Art in London to do
a Master's degree in 3D design

1994 Designs and builds the Gazebo at Sir Terence
Conran's home
Graduates from RCA
Founds Heatherwick Studio
Makes his first Christmas card

1997 Designs 'Autumn Intrusion' window display for Harvey Nichols
Wins his first big award

2000 Designs the vents at Paternoster Square

2002 Designs Bleigiessen, a giant glass
sculpture for the Wellcome Trust

2004 The Zip Bag is launched for French company,
Longchamp
Becomes the youngest-ever designer to be appointed a
Royal Designer for Industry

2005 The Rolling Bridge opens
Winner of Structural Steel Award
Winner of International Footbridge Award
Designs the East Beach Café, Littlehampton

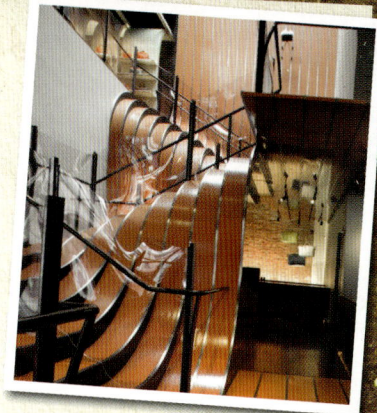

2006 Designs Longchamp's store in New York
Winner of the Prince Philip Designers Prize

2007 Wins the competition to design the British Pavilion
for the Shanghai Expo 2010
East Beach Café opens; it wins more than 20 awards

2008 Designs and builds 16 artists' studios at Aberystwyth

2010 Designs new London bus
Shanghai Expo: UK pavilion wins top prize, gold
medal for pavilion design

2011 Designs river boat in Nantes, France

2012 New bus for London goes into service
Olympic Cauldron is lit at the London Olympics

2013 Awarded CBE (Commander of the Order of the
British Empire) for services to the design industry

ARE YOU WONDERING WHAT THOMAS AND HIS STUDIO HAVE
DONE SINCE THEN? WHY NOT CHECK THEM OUT ONLINE
AND SEE WHAT THEY'RE UP TO?

GLOSSARY

accessory: a bag, hat or other extra item that goes with an outfit

brief: the instructions given for a job or task

commissioner: the person or organization who needs and pays for a project

draftsmen: people who do drawings that are used to make buildings or machines

feedback: comments on drawings, models, etc. that help to improve the finished product

fibreglass: a strong, light, man-made material often used in boats and cars

fine artist: an artist who produces work (for example, a painting, drawing or sculpture) for beauty rather than its practical use

gazebo: a small building in a garden

hydraulic ram: a plunger, powered by water pressure, which moves in or out

lathe: a machine tool used to cut or polish a rotating piece of wood, plastic or metal

legacy: the importance of something from the past

molecule: one of the tiny particles that make up a material

origami: the Japanese art of folding paper into shapes

press: the collective noun for newspapers or journalists

product design: creating new objects to be sold to customers

scale: the size of something

silo: a tall tower used to store grain

substation: a place that transforms powerful electricity to a safer level and sends it on to businesses and homes

suspension system: springs and other devices that absorb shock waves from the ground, making vehicles travel more smoothly

terrain: ground

thesis: a long piece of writing, based on original research, and usually written as part of a course

showcase: to show the best qualities of something

viaduct: a bridge-like structure that carries a road or railway across a valley

INDEX

ABOUT THE AUTHOR

When I left university, I started work in a publishing company. I was an editor on books for people learning English as a foreign language. Later I moved to work on children's books and then became a writer. (Top tip: When you're a writer you can work at home and get up late in the morning.) The books I write are mainly non-fiction – about anything from sharks and mummies to volcanoes and the Moon. I enjoy finding out about new things. I live quite near London so, when I'm not working, I like going to plays, concerts or art exhibitions.

It was interesting learning about Thomas Heatherwick. I was lucky enough to meet him and his colleagues, and look around the studio. What hard-working, talented people they are! Good design is a wonderful thing and adds a buzz to life. From now on, I'm going to seek it out. I hope you will look for it, too.

Greg Foot, Series Editor

I've loved science ever since the day I took my papier mâché volcano into school. I filled it with far too much baking powder, vinegar and red food colouring, and WHOOSH! I covered the classroom ceiling in red goo. Now I've got the best job in the world: I present TV shows for the BBC, answer kids' science questions on YouTube, and make huge explosions on stage at festivals!

Working on TreeTops inFact has been great fun. There are so many brilliant books, and guess what ... they're all packed full of awesome facts! What's your favourite?